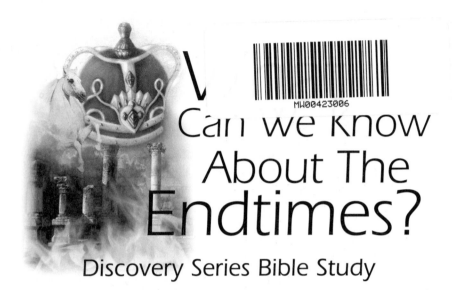

Can we know About The Endtimes?

Discovery Series Bible Study

Are the statements in the Bible about the future exact enough for us to know what lies ahead? Or are they too vague, too figurative, or too debatable to be of any real value to us today? What difference does it make whether or not we know ahead of time if it's all going to happen anyway? Let's look to the Bible for the answers to these and other important questions about the future.

Martin R. De Haan II, President of RBC Ministries

Publisher:	Discovery House Publishers
Editor:	David Sper
Graphic Design:	Alex Soh, Janet Chim, Felix Xu
Cover Photo & Illustration:	Ron Kimball (Horse), Jearn Ko (Crown), Bill Crowder (Ruins), Alex Soh (Sky)
Series Coordinator/Study Guide:	Bill Crowder, Sim Kay Tee

This *Discovery Series Bible Study* is based on the *Discovery Series* booklet *"What Can We Know About The Endtimes?"* (Q1201) from RBC Ministries. The *Discovery Series* has more than 140 titles on a variety of biblical and Christian-living issues. These 32-page booklets offer a rich resource of insight for your study of God's Word. For a catalog of *Discovery Series* booklets, write to RBC Ministries, PO Box 2222, Grand Rapids, MI 49501-2222 or visit us on the Web at: www.discoveryseries.org

Discovery House Publishers

A member of the RBC Ministries family:
Our Daily Bread, Day Of Discovery, RBC Radio, Discovery Series, Campus Journal, Discovery House Music, Sports Spectrum

ISBN 1-57293-093-4

Table Of Contents

Expectations

A woman in her 9th month of pregnancy.
A college student the week before final exams.
A teenager before his first date.
A man and woman as they say, "I do."
A patient who has been told he has cancer.
A criminal awaiting the judge's sentence.

Do your expectations turn out to be naively optimistic, unduly pessimistic, or surprisingly realistic? In most cases, what makes the difference is whether you acted on the basis of specific knowledge or on unfounded feelings.

Opinions about the future follow the same pattern. To avoid being victimized by false hopes or unrealistic fears, we need to search out reliable information and live by it.

> **To avoid being victimized by false hopes or unrealistic fears, we need to search out reliable information and live by it.**

Many find it hard to know whom to believe. Some predict a nuclear holocaust. Others speak ominously of mass starvation. Many economists are forecasting a worldwide financial collapse. Still others see a peaceful utopia just ahead.

Here are a few excerpts from actual conversations with people who expressed their hopes and fears about the endtimes.

- *"I heard some guy on TV talk about the book of Revelation, and it really spooked me."*
- *"I believe that I will see the end of the earth in my lifetime."*
- *"I don't see why Jesus would have to come back. If He was the Messiah, He would have done it right then."*
- *"If the judgment day comes, then I'm going to hell. I enjoy doing the things I'm doing wrong."*
- *"It's kind of scary to think that the world is going to come to an end someday, but if I have faith there is nothing to be afraid of."*
- *"I think everybody has the same destiny."*
- *"The future kind of scares me. I'm afraid of World War III and things like that."*
- *"I think God cares, but I don't think He's controlling things. I think He sees what happens and He hopes for the best."*
- *"I believe that God controls the future and that Jesus Christ will return just as He promised. I believe in an actual heaven and hell."*

Who's right? Which expectations are in line with what we can know for sure? In this study, we will be looking to the Bible for answers to our questions about the endtimes.

The Countdown Continues

No amount of effort can stop the clock of history. No mortal, no matter how influential, wealthy, or well-known can break the tyranny of time. Every day that passes, every flash of a digital crystal, brings us closer to the dramatic events predicted in the Bible. We can prepare for the inevitable. We can put time to good use. But we cannot stop it. Not for a moment.

That can be an unsettling thought. The prophetic passages of the Bible are filled with frightening scenes and complicated symbols. There are predictions of the sun going dark and the moon turning to blood. Four terrible horsemen are pictured as riding forth over the earth bringing war, famine, disease, and death. A blasphemous beast will rise out of the sea to shake his fist in the face of God and to bring untold suffering to God's children. A final, cataclysmic war will be fought, and blood will flow 5 feet deep in a valley 200 miles long. Finally, peace will settle over the earth like the warm, benevolent sunshine of spring.

These are frightening, confusing images. And when we read about prophecy, we come across technical terms like the great tribulation, the abomination of desolation, the return of Jesus Christ, the great white throne judgment, and the lake of fire.

What's ahead? How much can we know about the endtimes? Well, not everything, certainly. But the Bible does give us much information. In the pages that follow, we will identify and explain the seven major events of the endtimes.

Christ: Key To The Future

Christ is the center of God's plan for the endtimes.

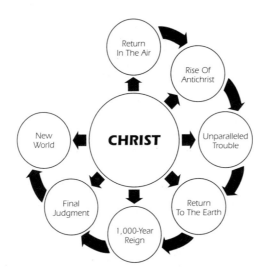

1. **Return In The Air:** Christ comes back for His own.
2. **Rise Of The Antichrist:** Christ is challenged.
3. **Unparalleled Trouble:** Christ troubles the nations and Israel.
4. **Return To The Earth:** Christ comes to rescue and judge Israel, and to judge the nations.
5. **1,000-Year Reign:** Christ rules the world from an earthly throne.
6. **Final Judgment:** Christ defeats His enemies and judges unbelievers.
7. **New World:** Christ creates a new heaven and a new earth.

STUDY NO. *1*

Setting The Stage

Hebrews 9:28—"Christ was offered once to bear the sins of many. To those who eagerly wait for Him He will appear a second time, apart from sin, for salvation."

Objective:
To understand an overview of the prophetic picture.

Bible Memorization:
Hebrews 9:28

Reading:
**"Expectations,"
"The Countdown Continues,"
"Christ: Key To The Future"
pp.4-7**

Warming Up
Everyone tends to be curious and fascinated about future events. Why do you think this is true? Where do people usually turn to find out about the future?

Thinking Through
What does the word *endtimes* make you think about? Why should Christians be concerned about endtime events? What difference does it make whether or not we know about endtime events?

A variety of opinions expressing people's hopes and fears about the endtimes are listed on page 5. What other opinions have you heard, and how did you respond to them?

Of the seven stages of future events listed on page 7, which one do you find most confusing? Most frightening? Most comforting? In each case, why?

Digging In
Key Text: John 14:1-3
What circumstances surround Jesus' declaration of comfort in these verses? Where and when does He say these words, and how does that context help us to understand His words?

Why does Jesus connect our present peace of mind to His promises about future events?

Notice how many times Jesus uses the personal pronoun "I." How are these promises linked to what Christ Himself will accomplish? Why is His credibility important to our present peace of mind and expectations for the future?

Going Further
Refer
In what ways is Christ the "key to the future"? (see Dan. 7:13-14; Mt. 24:30-31; 25:31-34; Jn. 14:3,6; Rev. 1:17-18).

Why must Christ come to earth a second time? (see Mt. 25:31-34; Mk. 13:31; Lk. 21:27-28; Acts 1:11; Heb. 9:28).

Reflect
In John 14:1-3, notice how many times Jesus uses the word *you* to personalize His promises. To what extent do you experience this peace that He has promised? Have you embraced these words of promise in your own heart? If not, will you now?

[1] "Let not your heart be troubled; you believe in God, believe also in Me. [2] In My Father's house are many mansions; if it were not so, I would have told you. I go to prepare a place for you. [3] And if I go and prepare a place for you, I will come again and receive you to Myself; that where I am, there you may be also."
John 14:1-3

Christ will Return In The Air

Because Christ can be trusted, we know that He will keep His promise to return for His own. He promised His disciples: "I go to prepare a place for you. And if I go and prepare a place for you, I will come again and receive you to Myself; that where I am, there you may be also" (Jn. 14:2-3).

What Will Happen?

This event is described in 1 Thessalonians 4:

> The Lord Himself will descend from heaven with a shout, with the voice of an archangel, and with the trumpet of God. And the dead in Christ will rise first. Then we who are alive and remain shall be caught up together with them in the clouds to meet the Lord in the air (vv.16-17).

At a predetermined time, the Son of God will leave the Father's side and descend toward earth. As He does, three mighty sounds will echo across the halls of heaven and sweep over the earth: a shout, the voice of an archangel, and a blast from the trumpet of God. When these sounds are heard, all believers since the time of Christ will be resurrected. The bodies of the Christians who have died will arise, be transformed, be reunited with their souls, and be taken to Christ's side in the air. Then every living Christian will be removed from the earth, "caught up" to join with the resurrected believers for a great and glorious meeting in the air. Christ will take them to be with Himself, and they will "always be with the Lord" (v.17).

This is also in view in 1 Corinthians 15:51-52, where Paul wrote:

> We shall not all sleep, but we shall all be changed—in a moment, in the twinkling of an eye, at the last trumpet. For the trumpet will sound, and the dead will be raised incorruptible, and we shall be changed.

In a moment of time the earth will be emptied of Christians.

When Will It Take Place?

No one really knows when this event will occur. The time is not spelled out in prophecy. We are told instead to maintain an attitude and condition of readiness, for Christ said:

> Therefore you also be ready, for the Son of Man is coming at an hour you do not expect (Mt. 24:44).

Christ taught this attitude of watchfulness in two similar parables recorded in Luke 12. In the first parable (vv.35-40), He likened His coming to the return of the master of the house from a wedding. In the second (vv.42-48), a man has left his household affairs in the hands of a servant.

The key element in both parables is that the day of the master's return could not be known. Because of that, the servants were to maintain constant readiness. The same is true of us as we wait for Christ's return.

This could occur at any moment. That's what the word *imminent* means. But that does not necessarily mean His return will occur soon. Yes, it's *imminent*— it could take place before you take your next breath, but it is not necessarily *immediate*. The Lord could delay His return another few hundred years.

We believe that this event will be the first of the endtime events. It is referred to as "the rapture of the church." The word *rapture* comes from the Latin word *rapere*, which literally means "to seize" or "to catch away." For an explanation of why we believe that the rapture is separate from the second coming of Christ to the earth, see pages 35-36.

The Judgment Seat Of Christ

Those who are taken from the earth will meet Christ in the clouds and go to be with Him. Then they will stand before the Lord in judgment. This event is called the judgment seat of Christ. Paul foresaw it when he wrote:

> We must all appear before the judgment seat of Christ, that each one may receive the things done in the body, according to what he has done, whether good or bad (2 Cor. 5:10).

The issue for those at the judgment seat of Christ will not be salvation. They are all God's children—forgiven and adopted on the basis of their acceptance of Christ. The purpose is to determine the degree of reward they receive. They will be called into account and receive what is due them (2 Cor. 5:10). The primary issue will be faithfulness (1 Cor. 4:2,4). This is emphasized in three of our Lord's parables: the worker in the vineyard (Mt. 20:1-16), the talents (Mt. 25:14-30), and the 10 minas (Lk. 19:11-27).

The issue for those at the judgment seat of Christ will not be salvation. . . . The purpose is to determine the degree of reward they receive.

Some will receive reward at the judgment seat of Christ; others will suffer loss (1 Cor. 3:11-15). We are not told just what this will involve. There will be no punishment, for Jesus Christ bore all the penalty for our sin on the cross. We may be shown our shortcomings and failures. We may be reminded of our selfishness and of the sins we did not confess. The "loss" we suffer will be in the receiving of less reward than we could have received.

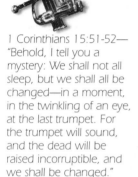

STUDY
NO. 2

What Can We Know?
Christ Will Return In The Air

1 Corinthians 15:51-52—
"Behold, I tell you a mystery: We shall not all sleep, but we shall all be changed—in a moment, in the twinkling of an eye, at the last trumpet. For the trumpet will sound, and the dead will be raised incorruptible, and we shall be changed."

Objective:
To understand the Bible's teachings about the rapture and the judgment seat of Christ.

Bible Memorization:
1 Corinthians 15:51-52

Reading:
**"Christ Will Return In The Air"
pp.10-13**

Warming Up
What would you do if you awoke one morning to find that a loved one in your family had disappeared— suddenly and unexpectedly—without a trace?

Thinking Through
On page 11, we are told of three mighty sounds that will sweep the earth at Christ's return for His children. What are they, and what do you think is their significance?

What is the key element of the two parables of watchfulness discussed on page 12? How can that key element affect the way we live for Christ each day?

How does the judgment seat of Christ fit into the prophetic scheme? (p.13). What will the primary issue of that judgment be? What is meant by "rewards" and "loss" at this judgment? (see also 1 Cor. 3:11-15; 9:24-27).

Digging In
Key Text: 1 Thessalonians 4:16-17
The context of the passage is that Paul is answering a question posed by believers who had seen loved ones taken in death. How did these words of Christ's return help them to fulfill the challenge of verse 18?

The phrase "we who are alive" reveals Paul's conviction about the imminence of Christ's return. What was that conviction, and why should we share it today?

Paul said to "comfort one another with these words" (v.18). How does the promise of the rapture comfort you? What hope does the rapture hold for those whose Christian loved ones have already died?

Going Further
Refer
Using a concordance, study Bible, Bible dictionary, or Bible encyclopedia, find Bible passages that speak about the different kinds of rewards that a Christian can expect to receive at the judgment seat of Christ. (Hint: Look for keywords like *crown* or *reward*.)

Reflect
Are you ready at this moment to appear before Christ's judgment seat? What do you think the Lord would say to you? (see Mt. 25:21,26). What rewards do you think you would receive from Him?

What changes in your life are needed so that you will not be ashamed to stand before Christ at His judgment seat? (Mt. 24:36-46).

[16] "The Lord Himself will descend from heaven with a shout, with the voice of an archangel, and with the trumpet of God. And the dead in Christ will rise first. [17] Then we who are alive and remain shall be caught up together with them in the clouds to meet the Lord in the air. And thus we shall always be with the Lord."
1 Thessalonians 4:16-17

The Antichrist Will Rise To Power

According to Bible prophecy, the next event on the endtime calendar is the rise of a false christ to world prominence. He is called the Antichrist.

The apostle John said that many false christs would appear (1 Jn. 2:18; 4:3). Claiming to be the Messiah, they will seek and attract many people. Some had already appeared while John was still alive. One day, however, the ultimate impostor will come. He will gather a huge following. He will deceive Israel into signing a false peace treaty (Dan. 9:27). And he will be the cause of untold suffering in the world, especially for the saints.

Here is what the Bible tells us about Antichrist:

- He will receive power from Satan (Rev. 13:2).
- He will receive his throne from Satan (Rev. 13:2).
- He will receive his authority from Satan (Rev. 13:2).
- He will be a ruler (Rev. 6:2).
- His purpose will be conquest (Rev. 6:2).
- He will be guilty of terrible blasphemy (Rev. 13:5).
- He will make a peace treaty with Israel and then cruelly break it (Dan. 9:27).
- He will put himself above everything and everyone (Dan. 11:37).
- He will proclaim himself to be God (2 Th. 2:4).
- He will stage a miraculous "resurrection" (Rev. 13:3).
- He will make war with the saints (Rev. 13:7).
- He will have authority over the nations (Rev. 13:7).
- His number is 666 (Rev. 13:18).
- He will kill millions of believers (Rev. 6:9-11; 7:9-17).
- A false prophet will serve him (Rev. 19:20).
- He will demand that his image be worshiped (Rev. 13:14).

16

The Antichrist is Satan's counterfeit. As Jesus Christ was sent by the Father, so this false christ will be sent by Satan. The Antichrist is given various descriptive names in the Bible. For example, he is referred to as:

- The Little Horn (Dan. 7:7-28).
- The King Of Fierce Countenance (Dan. 8:23-25).
- The Prince Who Is To Come (Dan. 9:26-27).
- The Willful King (Dan. 11:16,36-38).
- The Man Of Sin (2 Th. 2:3-4).
- The Son Of Perdition (2 Th. 2:3-4).
- The Beast (Rev. 13:1-10).

The Earth Will Experience Unparalleled Trouble

When the Antichrist is revealed, the stage will be set for the terrible events of the tribulation. After this satanically empowered leader rises to prominence, the stage will be set for the most distressing period of all history. For 3½ years he will conduct a reign of terror, bringing death to multitudes, both Jew and Gentile. But in addition to this reign of terror, the earth will experience unparalleled trouble as God's wrath is poured out on all mankind (Isa. 13:6-11).

The Nations Troubled

The nations will not go unpunished by the hand of God. They will live to hate the day they cast their lot with God's archenemy. For generations their leaders will have rejected God and mocked His Son. A just punishment will befall them in the 7-year period called "the tribulation."

Two sections of the New Testament describe the events of these 7 years: Matthew 24 and Revelation 6–16. These prophetic details indicate how mankind will suffer during this frightening time:

Matthew 24

- false christs
- wars
- rumors of war
- nation against nation
- famines

- earthquakes
- killing
- betrayal
- flight
- pestilences

Revelation 6–16

The Seals (Rev. 6)
1. Antichrist
2. war
3. famine
4. death
5. martyrdom
6. global destruction
7. the trumpets begin

The Trumpets (Rev. 8–9)
1. vegetation destroyed
2. death at sea
3. fresh water poisoned
4. the heavens struck
5. terrible locusts
6. death by demons
7. the bowl judgments begin

The Bowls (Rev. 15–16)
1. ugly sores
2. death of marine life
3. fresh water contaminated
4. unbearable heat
5. darkness and pain
6. demonic hordes
7. earthquake and hail

The suffering and death that will fall on the nations during the tribulation is indescribably horrible. Millions upon millions will die in the terrible outpouring of God's wrath. Yet the majority will not repent. Though they "gnawed their tongues" in agony, they will continue to curse the God of heaven and refuse to trust in Him (Rev. 16:10-11). There will be a great multitude of Gentiles, however, who will turn to God during the tribulation. John refers to them as "a great multitude which no one could number, of all nations, tribes, peoples, and tongues" (Rev. 7:9).

Israel Troubled

There are actually two purposes for the 7 years of tribulation. The first, as we have already seen, is the punishment of the nations. A second is to bring Israel to the place where she can be restored to the position of spiritual favor she once held in God's eyes. Israel will suffer with the nations—only more intensely. This is "the time of Jacob's trouble" prophesied by Jeremiah:

> Alas! For that day is great, so that none is like it; and it is the time of Jacob's trouble, but he shall be saved out of it (Jer. 30:7).

The tribulation will be a time of suffering and death for all mankind. But the Jews will be the hardest hit by the terror of those awful days. Zechariah predicted that two-thirds of all Jews on earth will die during the tribulation (13:8-9). But the suffering will bring Israel to repentance.

The prophet Ezekiel described Israel's conversion with these beautiful words:

> I will take you from among the nations, gather you out of all countries, and bring you into your own land. Then I will sprinkle clean water on you, and you shall be clean; I will cleanse you from all your filthiness and from all your idols. I will give you a new heart and put a new spirit within you; I will take the heart of stone out of your flesh and give you a heart of flesh. I will put My Spirit within you and cause you to walk in My statutes, and you will keep My judgments and do them. Then you shall dwell in the land that I gave to your fathers; you shall be My people, and I will be your God (Ezek. 36:24-28).

Biblical descriptions of Israel's restoration are also given in Ezekiel 37 (the valley of dry bones) and Zechariah 12:10-11.

The spiritual restoration of Israel as a nation will take place at the return of Jesus Christ to earth at the end of the tribulation. When He returns to rescue them from being annihilated by the Antichrist, they will nationally accept Him as their Messiah and Savior, even though individually a large number of Jews will already have been converted (Rev. 7:1-8).

After hundreds of generations of hardhearted disbelief, the people of Israel will trust in Jesus Christ as their true Messiah. In terrible agony, inflicted by the Antichrist, they will turn in faith to the Lord Jesus. This brings us to the next event in God's program for the endtimes, the return of Jesus Christ to earth.

STUDY
NO. 3

What Can We Know?

The Antichrist & Unparalleled Trouble

1 John 4:3—"Every spirit that does not confess that Jesus Christ has come in the flesh is not of God. And this is the spirit of the Antichrist, which you have heard was coming, and is now already in the world."

Objective:
To learn more about the person identified as the Antichrist and the 7-year period of tribulation on the earth.

Bible Memorization:
1 John 4:3
Reading:
"The Antichrist Will Rise" & "The Earth Will Experience"
pp.16-19

Warming Up
From movies to pulpits to politics, there has been much speculation about the identity of the Antichrist. Why is there so much interest in this topic? What world leaders or celebrities in recent history have been suspected of being the Antichrist? What reasons have been given?

Thinking Through
On page 16, we are told of a significant event involving the Antichrist and his relationship with Israel. What is it, and how would such an event be received in today's world?

What are the three series of judgments that will trouble the world after Antichrist's appearance? What will be the results of these judgments? (p.18).

What is the purpose of the time of trouble for the nation of Israel? (pp.18-19). Why do you think such suffering is necessary to accomplish this goal?

Digging In
Key Text: 2 Thessalonians 2:3-8
Why are the terms "man of sin" and "son of perdition" (v.3) appropriate for a false Christ sent by Satan?

20

According to verses 5 and 6, the Thessalonians knew what was restraining the "man of sin." What do you think is the identity of the restrainer mentioned in verse 7? How is this restraining being accomplished? What did Paul mean when he said the restrainer would be "taken out of the way"? (v.7).

What is the fate awaiting the Antichrist or "lawless one"? (v.8). How does the fact that his fate is already predetermined and sealed give us comfort or assurance?

Going Further

Refer

What did Paul mean in verse 7 when he warned that "the mystery of lawlessness is already at work"?

What are some of the works of the antichrists that are already seen in the world? (see 1 Jn. 2:18,22; 4:3; 2 Jn. 1:7). How do these things affect the life and witness of Christians today?

Reflect

A believer considering the terrors of the tribulation and the Antichrist should have at least two responses: thankfulness for salvation and concern for the lost who will go through this terrible time on the earth. In what ways does knowledge of the endtimes help us to share Christ with those who don't know Him?

³ "Let no one deceive you by any means; for that Day will not come unless the falling away comes first, and the man of sin is revealed, the son of perdition, ⁴ who opposes and exalts himself above all that is called God or that is worshiped, so that he sits as God in the temple of God, showing himself that he is God. ⁵ Do you not remember that when I was still with you I told you these things? ⁶ And now you know what is restraining, that he may be revealed in his own time. ⁷ For the mystery of lawlessness is already at work; only He who now restrains will do so until He is taken out of the way. ⁸ And then the lawless one will be revealed, whom the Lord will consume with the breath of His mouth and destroy with the brightness of His coming."

2 Thessalonians 2:3-8

Christ Will Return
To The Earth

As the tribulation draws to a close, the earth will be in turmoil. Millions will have died in war or its aftermath. The Antichrist's hatred of God will focus on the Jews as the 7 years reach their conclusion.

Opposed from the north and east (Dan. 11:44-45), the Antichrist will march his armies into Palestine in preparation for a vast military showdown. Evil spirits will draw the nations together for a final battle on the plains of Megiddo (Rev. 16:12-16).

The armies assembled in Palestine will be made up of bloodthirsty men who have resisted God throughout the tribulation. Both sides—the Antichrist and his opponents—will hate the people of God. They will engage in a fierce battle at Armageddon. The fighting will reach Jerusalem, and the Jews living there will suffer horribly (Zech. 14:1-2). A sense of despair will sweep over them as both armies attack them.

Suddenly, when all seems hopeless, the scene will change. Jesus Christ will appear in all His glory and descend to the Mount of Olives. When His feet touch it, the mountain will split in half, forming a vast new valley stretching from the Jordan River to the Mediterranean Sea (Zech. 14:3-9). The Jewish believers will be given superhuman strength to fight the Lord's enemies (Zech. 12:6-9), God will send a plague on the enemy soldiers and their animals (Zech. 14:12,15), and panic will grip the foreign troops, causing them to attack one another (Zech. 14:13).

In Revelation 19:11-21, the apostle John provides us with a beautiful portrait of Christ's second coming. He is depicted astride a white horse, His eyes blazing. The Antichrist will rally the armies of earth to attack Him, but they will be crushed in defeat. Israel will be rescued. The armed hordes of earth will be slain. The Antichrist and his cohort will be thrown into the lake of fire. Satan himself will be bound. And the victorious Christ will prepare to ascend His throne in Jerusalem to rule in peace for 1,000 years.

Those Who Survive The Tribulation

Jesus Christ will hold two special judgments at the close of the tribulation. The first will be for the Jews who survive those terrible days. The prophet Ezekiel described the Lord Jesus as a shepherd standing at the door of a sheepfold. The Jews who have trusted Him will be received into His kingdom; those who rejected Him will not (Ezek. 20:33-44).

> **Believers in Christ (the sheep) will be allowed
> to enter the millennial kingdom;
> unbelievers (the goats) will die and await
> the great white throne judgment.**

A similar judgment will be held for the Gentiles who live through the tribulation. Again, a shepherd metaphor is used to describe Christ. He is pictured as separating the sheep from the goats (Mt. 25:31-46). Believers in Christ (the sheep) will be allowed to enter the millennial kingdom; unbelievers (the goats) will die and await the great white throne judgment (see p.29).

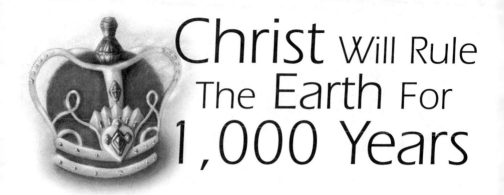

Christ Will Rule The Earth For 1,000 Years

The battle is over. The armed hordes of the earth have been defeated. Just when all seemed lost, Jesus Christ appeared in glory, leading His armies to earth. Before the day ended, the Battle of Armageddon had been won by Him. But the earth is in ruins. Death and destruction lie everywhere. What will happen?

Rather than returning to His Father in heaven, Jesus Christ will erect His throne in Jerusalem, establish it as His capital city, reinstate the Jews as His people, and rule over the entire earth in a 1,000-year reign of peace, prosperity, and righteousness, which we call the millennium (Rev. 20:4-6).

The Old Testament prophecies are filled with details about the new government Christ will establish when He returns. Here is what it will be like when the Lord Jesus rules the world:

1. Christ Will Be King.

- The Branch of David will rule (Jer. 23:5).
- Christ will fulfill His prophesied rule (Lk. 1:32-33).
- The believers of the church age will reign with Christ (Rev. 20:4,6).

2. Israel Will Be Prominent.

- Israel will be the favored nation (Isa. 2:1-3).
- Jerusalem will be the capital city (Isa. 60:10-14).
- David's throne will be reestablished (Lk. 1:32).

3. Christ's Rule Will Reflect His Character.

- Justice for everyone (Isa. 2:4).
- All will prosper (Mic. 4:4).
- He will reign in righteousness (Jer. 23:5).
- The earth will be at peace (Zech. 8:4-5).
- People will be safe (Jer. 23:5-6).

4. The Natural World Will Be Transformed.

- Climate will be ideal (Isa. 30:23-26).
- Wild animals will be tame (Isa. 11:6-8).
- Fishing will be great (Ezek. 47:9-10).
- People will have good health (Isa. 35:5-6).
- Life will be lengthened (Isa. 65:19-20,22).
- Trees will provide food and medicine (Ezek. 47:12).

5. God Will Be Worshiped.

- His name will be known throughout the world (Mal. 1:11).
- The temple at Jerusalem will be the center of worship (Ezek. 40–48).
- Representatives will come from everywhere (Zech. 14:16).
- All mankind will come (Isa. 66:23).
- The Jews will lead in worship (Isa. 60:10-14).

When Christ rules in the millennial kingdom, His love, justice, mercy, righteousness, and peace will be found throughout the earth. Since people reflect their ruler, the people of the kingdom will reflect the characteristics of their King. During this golden age, the earth will be what God intended it to be.

Warming Up

What images does the word *Armageddon* conjure up in your mind? Do you think Armageddon will be World War III? Why or why not?

What Can We Know?

Christ Returns In The Air & Christ Will Rule

Matthew 25:31—"When the Son of Man comes in His glory, and all the holy angels with Him, then He will sit on the throne of His glory."

Thinking Through

Jesus will come to rescue Israel from the armies of the world at the Battle of Armageddon (p.24). The word *Armageddon* is often used to refer to the end of the world, but what's the biblical view of that great battle?

What two special judgments follow the close of the tribulation? (p.23). Who is involved in these judgments? How do they differ from the judgment seat of Christ?

What are the five main characteristics of the millennium, the earthly kingdom of Christ? (pp.24-25). Why can these things happen only when Christ personally reigns on the earth?

Digging In
Key Text: Revelation 20:4-6

What is the fate awaiting Satan? (vv.1-3). Why is he bound for 1,000 years? What would life be like without Satan's influence on the earth?

How many times is 1,000 years referred to in this text? Is it more reasonable to think that this is a symbolic or literal period of time? Why?

According to verses 4-6, who will reign with Christ during His millennial kingdom? Who else will share in that reign? (see 1 Cor. 6:2; 2 Tim. 2:12; Rev. 1:6; 5:10).

Going Further
Refer
Using a concordance, study Bible, Bible dictionary, or Bible encyclopedia, list some other Scripture passages that refer to the millennial rule of Christ.

Reflect
People of every generation have longed to see this world rescued from conflict and strife, and brought into a condition of peace and harmony. Though this will happen perfectly when Christ rules in His kingdom, what can we do now to be peacemakers in our strife-torn world?

Does the fact that you will sit on a throne and reign with Christ threaten or encourage you? Why is it possible for us to share in this privilege?

[4] "I saw thrones, and they sat on them, and judgment was committed to them. Then I saw the souls of those who had been beheaded for their witness to Jesus and for the word of God, who had not worshiped the beast or his image, and had not received his mark on their foreheads or on their hands. And they lived and reigned with Christ for a thousand years. [5] But the rest of the dead did not live again until the thousand years were finished. This is the first resurrection. [6] Blessed and holy is he who has part in the first resurrection. Over such the second death has no power, but they shall be priests of God and of Christ, and shall reign with Him a thousand years."
Revelation 20:4-6

Christ Will Judge Unbelievers

At the end of the 1,000-year reign of Christ on the earth, Satan, who had been locked up during this time, will be released. Immediately gathering a gigantic army of unbelievers together, Satan will lead them in battle against the Lord. This will be Satan's final act of rebellion.

All Rebellion Abolished

John's description is in Revelation 20:7-10.

> When the thousand years have expired, Satan will be released from his prison and will go out to deceive the nations which are in the four corners of the earth, Gog and Magog, to gather them together to battle, whose number is as the sand of the sea. They went up on the breadth of the earth and surrounded the camp of the saints and the beloved city. And fire came down from God out of heaven and devoured them. The devil, who deceived them, was cast into the lake of fire and brimstone where the Beast and the False Prophet are. And they will be tormented day and night forever and ever.

It had all begun sometime in eternity past, when Lucifer had looked with a jealous eye at the throne of God. In pride he led a rebellion of angels against God and was cast out of heaven (Isa. 14:12-14; Ezek. 28:12-15). From the time of his deception in the Garden until he was cast into the bottomless pit, he has brought immeasurable suffering to mankind. Now, after 1,000 years of confinement, his hatred of God has intensified. He makes one last, desperate attempt to dethrone the Lord. But in spite of all of his power, his fate will be the same as his wicked underlings, the Antichrist and the False Prophet—everlasting torment in hell.

All Unbelievers Judged

When Satan's last rebellion is smashed, it will be time for the final judgment. A new heaven and a new earth will soon be appearing, and the last details of earth-business must be taken care of. This judgment will occur at the great white throne of God (Rev. 20:11-15).

We are told that "the dead, small and great," (v.12) will stand before the throne. Unbelievers of Old Testament days, the church age, the tribulation, and the millennium will be there as the books are opened. No one will escape, for "the sea . . . and Death and Hades" (v.13) will give up their inhabitants. The outcome will not be in question. Those who rejected God's offer of salvation in Christ will have sealed their own fate. Their names will not be found in the Lamb's Book of Life. They will be cast into the lake of fire, which is already inhabited by Satan, Antichrist, and the False Prophet. This is the second death—eternal death.

"God is not vengeful or capricious.
His judgment stems from His holiness."

These are not pleasant thoughts. We don't like the idea of eternal suffering. The idea of flames and anguish appalls us. But remember, these are people who intentionally and willfully chose not to trust in Christ. They turned their backs on God's grace, deciding to leave Him out of their lives. It was their own choice.

God is not vengeful and capricious. He does not cause suffering just for the sport of it. His judgment stems from His holiness, and He is absolutely righteous and holy. No one will receive one bit more or less than he deserves, because God can only judge rightly.

When questions of eternal suffering disturb us, let's remember the words of Abraham: "Shall not the Judge of all the earth do right?" (Gen.18:25). Then, in faith, we can leave it squarely in His hands.

A New World Will Be Created

We come now to the final event on God's prophetic timetable—which, like a commencement, is more of a beginning than an ending. That which begins with the new world will last from that point on—forever. From the ruins of the old heavens and earth, God will bring into existence an eternal new world free from evil, free from deceit, free from all the harmful, debilitating things that have marred the earth since Adam's sin.

The prophetic books are filled with information about the millennial kingdom, but they tell us very little about the new world to come. Most of our information comes from Revelation 21–22. It begins:

> I saw a new heaven and a new earth, for the first heaven and the first earth had passed away (Rev. 21:1).

What will happen to the old world-system? It will be burned to ashes in the aftermath of Satan's final attack (Rev. 20:7-10). Peter described it as follows:

> The day of the Lord will come as a thief in the night, in which the heavens will pass away with a great noise, and the elements will melt with fervent heat, but the earth and the works that are in it will be burned up (2 Pet. 3:10).

From these charred, smoking ruins, the Creator will bring into existence an eternal home of amazing beauty and grandeur for His own. As we consider the elements of this new world, we will be dazzled by the picture that appears in our minds.

The New Jerusalem

In his vision, John saw the holy city descend from heaven. He described it in Revelation 21 and 22 as follows:

- as beautiful as a bride dressed for her husband (21:2)
- where God dwells with men (21:3)
- immense in size (21:16)
- a jeweled foundation (21:19-20)
- a 216-foot-high wall of jasper (21:17-18)
- 12 gates of pearl, always open (21:21,25)
- buildings and streets of gold (21:18,21)
- illuminated by God's glory (21:11,23)
- a crystal river (22:1)
- trees of life for healing (22:2)
- the throne of God (22:3)

The city is also remarkable for what is not there. The following things will be missing from our heavenly home:

- no sea (21:1)
- no tears (21:4)
- no death (21:4)
- no pain (21:4)
- no sorrow (21:4)
- no temple (21:22)
- no sun (21:23)
- no moon (21:23)
- no impurity (21:27)
- no deceit (21:27)
- no more curse (22:3)
- no night (22:5)

What a wonderful place! There will be no night because our heavenly home will be illuminated by the glory of God, and the Lamb will be its light (21:23; 22:5). There will be no temple because Christ Himself will be the temple (21:22). We will reign there forever (22:5). We will see the face of God and bear His name on our foreheads (22:4). We will have access forever to the tree of life (22:2,14).

With this description of heaven complete, the Bible comes to an end. When we think of the wonders of that home awaiting us, where the Lord Himself will dwell with us, we can only say with John, "Even so, come, Lord Jesus!" (Rev. 22:20).

STUDY
NO. **5**

What Can We Know?

Christ Will Judge & A New World

Luke 10:20—
"Nevertheless do not rejoice in this, that the spirits are subject to you, but rather rejoice because your names are written in heaven."

Objective:
To recognize the difference between eternal life with Christ and eternal judgment.

Bible Memorization:
Luke 10:20

Reading:
"Christ Will Judge Unbelievers" & "A New World Will Be Created" pp.28-31

Warming Up

What are some of the popular images that have been associated with hell? How accurate do you think these pictures are? What emotions or fears do you have when you think of hell? Why?

Thinking Through

On pages 28-29, we are told that at the end of 1,000 years of a perfect environment on earth, Satan will lead a final rebellion against God. Why do you think people who have experienced the perfection of the millennial kingdom could so quickly be led into rebellion against a perfect King?

What is the great white throne judgment? (see p.29). Why is this judgment necessary? Who is judged, on what basis are they judged, and what is the outcome? How is this judgment different from the judgment seat of Christ?

The final portion of Revelation describes the creation of the new heavens and earth. In the list of things that will *not* be present in this perfect place (p.31), what is the most comforting to you? Why?

Digging In
Key Text: Revelation 21:1-4

How does the statement "no more sea" in verse 1 distinguish the eternal state from our present world?

Compare verse 3 with Genesis 1–2. How does this wonderful promise restore the relationship with God that was broken in the Garden of Eden?

According to verse 4, how will God personally care for and comfort His children throughout eternity in the New Jerusalem?

Going Further
Refer

Read Jesus' words in Luke 16:19-31. What insights can you gain about heaven and hell from this passage? What do these verses teach about unbelievers getting a second chance to hear and respond to the gospel after they die?

Reflect

What effect does the Bible's teaching about heaven and hell have on your motivation to tell people about the forgiveness that is available in Jesus Christ? Ask God to make you more aware of the people around you who need to hear the saving message of the gospel.

[1] "Now I saw a new heaven and a new earth, for the first heaven and the first earth had passed away. Also there was no more sea. [2] Then I, John, saw the holy city, New Jerusalem, coming down out of heaven from God, prepared as a bride adorned for her husband. [3] And I heard a loud voice from heaven saying, 'Behold, the tabernacle of God is with men, and He will dwell with them, and they shall be His people. God Himself will be with them and be their God. [4] And God will wipe away every tear from their eyes; there shall be no more death, nor sorrow, nor crying. There shall be no more pain, for the former things have passed away.'"
Revelation 21:1-4

What We Can't Know About The Endtimes

No biblical subject brings out the imagination in people more than prophecy. Some people look into the prophetic books and always seem to find things that are sensational. Often their conjectures cannot be supported—either by context or by content. We have been talking in this booklet about endtime events that we know will take place. Let's look now at four things we cannot know about the future, but that people often claim to have special knowledge about.

1. The Date Of Christ's Return.

Time and again, self-proclaimed prophets have used Bible statements to support their "findings" that Jesus will return on a certain day or in a certain year. Some of these charlatans have even persuaded their followers to sell their earthly goods, combine their financial resources, and head for the hills to await the Lord's return. But God's Word says clearly, "Therefore you also be ready, for the Son of Man is coming at an hour you do not expect" (Mt. 24:44).

Many Christians fell into the trap of date-setting after Israel became a nation in 1948. They based their conclusion on Matthew 24:32-34, which says that the generation who sees "the fig tree" bud "will by no means pass away till all these things [the events prior to and including Christ's return] take place." Since Israel is pictured as a fig tree in the Old Testament, many believed that the Lord would return within the next generation (40 years). This would date the coming of Christ to the earth sometime before 1988 and the rapture of the church before 1981— obviously not an accurate interpretation of the events.

2. The Identity Of Antichrist.

Whenever a popular world leader with charisma, charm, and intelligence appears on the scene, he is tagged by someone as the Antichrist. In a sense, the people who make this kind of prediction are on the right track. The one who will rise to international prominence during the tribulation will indeed have those

34

characteristics. We have no scriptural basis, however, for knowing beforehand who that man will be. That will only become evident when he is revealed to mankind during the tribulation.

3. The United States In Biblical Prophecy.

Some find it exciting to think that God may have given the United States special mention in His Book. They claim, for example, that Revelation 18 reveals the United States as commercial Babylon. Yet nothing in the passage specifically requires that conclusion. The evils it mentions are just as true of almost every other civilization on earth as they are of the United States.

4. Specific Details.

When prophetic experts go beyond what is clearly revealed in the Bible, they are only speculating. In other words, we have no biblical basis for saying that the world will run out of oil, that the United States faces a dictatorship, that paper money will be abolished, or that the number 666 is a computer number. There is a danger in seeing every current event as a fulfillment of prophecy. Details like these are not revealed in the Scriptures.

The Two Phases of Christ's Return

The endtimes are more easily understood when a distinction is made between the coming of Christ in the air to remove His church and the coming of Christ to the earth to rescue Israel and set up His kingdom. These are the two phases of Christ's return. This distinction is based on the following evidence:

1. Imminency.

The Bible clearly teaches that Christ could return at any time. But it also teaches that certain catastrophic events will take place during the tribulation, prior to His return—putting the Lord's people in a state of readiness and expectation. This problem can be resolved if the coming of Christ is seen in two phases. His coming in the air will be sudden and without warning, but His coming to the earth will be expected by those who are alive during the tribulation and who know the biblical record.

2. Israel And The Church.

Israel and the church are two distinct entities, with distinct makeup, identity, and destiny. Israel is a nation; the church is made up of people of all nations (including Israel) who put their faith in Christ. Israel is promised prosperity and fulfillment on earth; the church is promised blessings in heavenly places.

3. The Removal Of The Restrainer.

In 2 Thessalonians 2:7 we are told that the way will not be clear for last-day events until a "restrainer" is taken away. It seems very probable that this "restrainer" is the Holy Spirit as He indwells individual members of the church. The removal of these persons, referred to by Christ as the "salt of the earth" and the "light of the world," would clear the way for a worldwide deception.

4. Differing Descriptions Of Christ's Coming.

First Thessalonians 4:17 pictures Christ coming in the clouds to "catch up" His people to meet with Him in the air, but Zechariah 14:5 and Revelation 19:14 picture Him as coming to the earth with His people.

5. The Church Not Destined For God's Wrath.

Revelation 3:10 indicates that the church is not destined for "the hour of trial which shall come upon the whole world." Scripture speaks of "the time of Jacob's trouble" (Jer. 30:7) as that future time when Israel will be brought to her knees in preparation for the coming of her Messiah. Israel will suffer before her restoration, but 1 Thessalonians 5:9 indicates that the church will escape that day of God's wrath.

6. The State Of The Kingdom Inhabitants.

According to 1 Corinthians 15:51, all the righteous will be changed. And Matthew 25:41-46 says that all the unrighteous will be sent into everlasting punishment. If there were no distinction between the two phases of Christ's coming, only glorified, transformed believers would be left to inhabit the kingdom. This doesn't seem possible, because children will be born in the millennium (Isa. 11:6-8). And more important, who does Satan lead in worldwide rebellion against Christ at the end of the millennium if not those unbelievers born during the 1,000 years? Initially, only believers will inhabit the kingdom (Ezek. 20:33-44; Mt. 25:31-46).

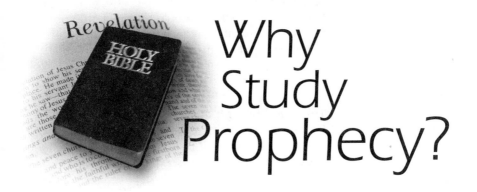

Why Study Prophecy?

1. It Promotes Love And Respect For God's Word.

An understanding of the Scriptures shows that God has fulfilled amazing prophecies in the past. This assures us that He will also fulfill those that predict the endtimes. Furthermore, a detailed study of the prophetic Scriptures is bound to give us a greater understanding of all Bible truth and a deeper appreciation for God's Word.

2. It Promotes Watchfulness And Purity.

It will motivate us to be ready for the any-moment return of Jesus Christ. Our Lord Himself emphasized this when He referred to Noah, to the faithful servant, to the 10 virgins, and to the talents (Mt. 24:36–25:30).

The apostle John exhorted us to be faithful, so that when our Lord appears we will be confident and unashamed (1 Jn. 2:28). He went on to say, "Everyone who has this hope in Him purifies himself, just as He is pure" (3:3).

3. It Promotes A Philosophy Of History.

Even though prophecy does not give us an exactly detailed prewritten history, it does lay out the future course for man and the earth. It tells us that the life God created on earth is worthwhile. It shows that God has specific plans for man and for our planet. He will correct the injustices; He will right the wrongs; He will rid the world of evil. The long, arduous course of human history will climax in a golden age of universal peace, prosperity, and righteousness that will exceed our fondest dreams.

STUDY
NO. 6

Considering The Facts

Matthew 24:44—
"Therefore you also be ready, for the Son of Man is coming at an hour you do not expect."

Objective:
To respond to critical issues about the overall scheme of endtime prophecy.

Bible Memorization:
Matthew 24:44

Reading:
**"What We Can't Know About The Endtimes," "The Two Phases Of Christ's Return," & "Why Study Prophecy?"
pp.34-37**

Warming Up
If you knew that Jesus would return at 3:00 p.m. this Wednesday, what would you be doing between now and then in anticipation of that event?

Thinking Through
People often claim that they have special knowledge about the endtimes. What are four things we cannot know about the future? (see pp.34-35).

Why is it necessary to see Christ's return in two phases? What evidence supports this view? (see pp.35-36). What is the meaning of *imminency*? How should a belief in the imminent return of Christ for His church affect the way Christians live?

Many people avoid studying prophecy for a variety of reasons, including fear or frustration. What three powerful reasons to study prophecy are given on page 37? Which of these reasons is the most motivating to you personally?

Digging In
Key Text: 1 John 3:1-3
The hope of the believer is found in the words of verse 2, "When He is revealed, we shall be like Him, for we shall see Him as He is." How does this parallel 1 Corinthians 15:51-58? What will happen to us at that meeting?

Contrast the way the world rejects the child of God to the way the Father accepts us (1 Jn. 3:1). How is this acceptance possible, and what are its results? (see Rom. 5:1-11).

According to verse 3, what is the result of living in the hope of Christ's return? What is our responsibility in achieving this result? What does this verse, along with 1 John 2:28, tell us about how to live so that we won't be ashamed when He returns?

Going Further
Refer
Compare 1 John 3:2 with Romans 8:28-29. What do these passages reveal to be God's purpose for each of His children? How is it achieved?

Reflect
We began this series of Bible lessons with the proposition that Christ is the key to endtime events (p.7). How has this been affirmed through this study?

God's ultimate desire for us is that we become like Christ. This process begins when we trust Christ as our personal Lord and Savior. Have you placed your faith in Jesus Christ for forgiveness of sins and eternal life? If so, spend several moments in thankful prayer for His gift of eternal life. If you have not trusted Him, will you do so now?

[1] "Behold what manner of love the Father has bestowed on us, that we should be called children of God! Therefore the world does not know us, because it did not know Him. [2] Beloved, now we are children of God; and it has not yet been revealed what we shall be, but we know that when He is revealed, we shall be like Him, for we shall see Him as He is. [3] And everyone who has this hope in Him purifies himself, just as He is pure."
1 John 3:1-3

"My Life Was Turned Around"

Clair Hess, senior editor of RBC Ministries, tells how his fear of the second coming of Christ was changed to joyful expectation through a correct understanding of the Bible teaching about endtime events.

One of the memories of my childhood and teen years is not pleasant; in fact, it is a recollection of fear. I remember actually trembling at the thought that the "end of the world" might be near.

I don't recall hearing much teaching as a boy about the rapture, the glorious appearing of Christ, or the millennium. Instead, the people I worshiped with placed an emphasis on the earth burning up with great heat, the sun being darkened, and the moon turning to blood. These images seared my mind with fear, dimmed my interest in the second coming, and drained any assurance I had that Christ would protect His own from the coming tribulation.

When I did hear a message about the Lord's return, I was afraid that I would be left behind. I came home one day after school and found no one there. I was petrified! I was sure that the Lord had come, and that I was the only one in my family who was left to face the horrors of the end of time. I had not been taught that because I had received Christ as my Savior I was really safe—for time and eternity.

Although I knew that heaven is the final home of the Christian (and surely everyone wanted to go there, not to the other place), it seemed that only old people spoke of it.

No one was really in any hurry to get there. Songs portrayed the beauties and wonders of the "home over there," but they were sung most often at funerals.

I was secretly hoping that Jesus would not come in my lifetime. I had too much I wanted to do. Living seemed more precious, more exciting, than being with Jesus.

"I was secretly hoping that Jesus would not come in my lifetime. I had too much I wanted to do. Living seemed more precious, more exciting, than being with Jesus."

After high school, I became interested in the Bible teaching I heard on the radio. I began attending summer gospel tent meetings. I bought a study Bible, and I started reading it with friends. An uncle helped me to understand the sequence of coming events in prophecy. My fears vanished as I read Titus 2:13, "Looking for the blessed hope and glorious appearing of our great God and Savior Jesus Christ."

I learned to live each day in the sure promise of John 14:1-3, where Jesus told us not to be troubled, that He is preparing a place for us, and that He will come back to take us to be with Him.

As I've grown older, some of my loved ones and friends have been called to their heavenly home. They have gone to be "with Christ, which is far better" (Phil. 1:23). I know the Lord more intimately now, and heaven seems much closer than it did before. I would be glad if He came today.

Christ, who loved me and gave Himself for me, is coming. It may be today! Life is more exhilarating now. Each day is an adventure. Yes, an understanding of God's program for the future has turned my life around.

What Does This Mean To Me?

We have answered the question, "What can we know about the endtimes?" Using the Bible as our guide, we have surveyed what God has revealed about the end of this age and the ages to come. We have looked in on scenes of indescribable bloodshed, horror, and death. And we have had a glimpse of bliss and goodness that surpasses human comprehension.

If you have trusted in Christ as your Lord and Savior, you can have confidence about the future. A day is coming, perhaps soon, when the Lord will return for you. Then you will return with Christ to share in His millennial rule. And after the thousand years are over, you will live with Him in a new world forever in a life of happiness and fulfillment that centers on the Lord Jesus.

> **If you have trusted in Christ as your Lord and Savior, you can have confidence about the future.**
> **If you haven't, the future is not so promising.**
> **The countdown continues. The time of opportunity is now. Make your decision. Trust Christ today.**

But if you are not a Christian, the future is not so promising. The wrath of God will be poured out on the earth, and on you, in a time of terrible war, disease, and famine. And beyond that lies the second death—a fate every bit as real for the unbeliever as heaven is for the person who trusts in Christ.

The countdown continues. The time of opportunity is now. Make your decision. Trust Christ today. Believing that He died to pay the penalty for your sins, ask Him to save you. He has promised that He would. Then, when you have done so, your future will be secure—both in this life and in the ages to come.

Discovery Series Bible Study Leader's And User's Guide

Statement Of Purpose

The *Discovery Series Bible Study* (DSBS) series provides assistance to pastors and leaders in discipling and teaching Christians through the use of RBC Ministries *Discovery Series* booklets. The DSBS series uses the inductive Bible-study method to help Christians understand the Bible more clearly.

Study Helps

Listed at the beginning of each study are the key verse, objective, and memorization verses. These will act as the compass and map for each study.

Some key Bible passages are printed out fully. This will help the students to focus on these passages and to examine and compare the Bible texts more easily—leading to a better understanding of their meanings. Serious students are encouraged to open their own Bible to examine the other Scriptures as well.

How To Use DSBS (for individuals and small groups)

Individuals—Personal Study
- Read the designated pages of the book.
- Carefully consider and answer all the questions.

Small Groups—Bible-Study Discussion
- To maximize the value of the time spent together, each member should do the lesson work prior to the group meeting.
- Recommended discussion time: 45–55 minutes.
- Engage the group in a discussion of the questions, seeking full participation from each of the members.

Overview Of Lessons

Study	Topic	Bible Text	Reading	Questions
1	Setting The Stage	Jn. 14:1-3	pp.4-7	pp.8-9
2	What Can We Know? (Part 1)	1 Th. 4:16-17	pp.11-13	pp.14-15
3	What Can We Know? (Part 2)	2 Th. 2:3-8	pp.16-19	pp.20-21
4	What Can We Know? (Part 3)	Rev. 20:4-6	pp.22-25	pp.26-27
5	What Can We Know? (Part 4)	Rev. 21:1-4	pp.28-31	pp.32-33
6	Considering The Facts	1 Jn. 3:1-3	pp.34-37	pp.38-39

The DSBS format incorporates a "layered" approach to Bible study that includes four segments. These segments form a series of perspectives that become increasingly more personalized and focused. These segments are:

Warming Up. In this section, a general interest question is used to begin the discussion (in small groups) or "to get the juices flowing" (in personal study). It is intended to begin the process of interaction at the broadest, most general level.

Thinking Through. Here, the student or group is invited to interact with the *Discovery Series* material that has been read. In considering the information and implications of the booklet, these questions help to drive home the critical concepts of that portion of the booklet.

Digging In. Moving away from the *Discovery Series* material, this section isolates a key biblical text from the manuscript and engages the student or group in a brief inductive study of that passage of Scripture. This brings the authority of the Bible into the forefront of the study as we consider its message to our hearts and lives.

Going Further. This final segment contains two parts. In *Refer*, the student or group has the opportunity to test the ideas of the lesson against the rest of the Bible by cross-referencing the text with other verses. In *Reflect*, the student or group is challenged to personally apply the lesson by making a practical response to what has been learned.

Pulpit Sermon Series (for pastors and church leaders)

Although the *Discovery Series Bible Study* is primarily for personal and group study, pastors may want to use this material as the foundation for a series of messages on this important issue. The suggested topics and their corresponding texts are as follows:

Sermon No.	Topic	Text
1	Setting The Stage	Jn. 14:1-3
2	The Rapture Of The Church	1 Th. 4:16-17
3	Antichrist And The Tribulation	2 Th. 2:3-8
4	Christ's Return And Kingdom	Rev. 20:4-6
5	Final Judgment And A New World	Rev. 21:1-4
6	Considering The Facts	1 Jn. 3:1-3

Final Thoughts

The DSBS will provide an opportunity for growth and ministry. To internalize the spiritual truths of each study in a variety of environments, the material is arranged to allow for flexibility in the application of the truths discussed.

Whether DSBS is used in small-group Bible studies, adult Sunday school classes, adult Bible fellowships, men's and women's study groups, or church-wide applications, the key to the strength of the discussion will be found in the preparation of each participant. Likewise, the effectiveness of personal and pastoral use of this material will be directly related to the time committed to using this resource.

As you use, teach, or study this material, may you "grow in the grace and knowledge of our Lord and Savior Jesus Christ" (2 Pet. 3:18).

Reflections

OUR DAILY BREAD

Delivered right to your home!

What could be better than getting *Our Daily Bread?* How about having it delivered directly to your home?

You'll also have the opportunity to receive special offers or Bible-study booklets. And you'll get articles written on timely topics we all face, such as forgiveness and anger.

To order your copy of *Our Daily Bread,* write to us at:

USA: PO Box 2222, Grand Rapids, MI 49501-2222
CANADA: Box 1622, Windsor, ON N9A 6Z7
RBC Web site: www.odb.org/guide

RBC Ministries
RADIO BIBLE CLASS ~ FOUNDED 1938

Support for RBC Ministries comes from the gifts of our members and friends. We are not funded or endowed by any group or denomination.